OXFORD & CAMBRIDGE

The histories of the county towns of Oxford and Cambridge extend back to the ninth century, as testified by Saxon records and monuments. In the Middle Ages both towns played a significant part in England's commercial life, with their great fairs and influential trade and craft guilds, but their later development was far less conventional.

For Oxford and Cambridge were destined to become famous throughout the civilised world as strongholds of learning and scholarship. Oxford's University College, Balliol and Merton and Cambridge's Peterhouse were all founded in the thirteenth century and, when Queen Elizabeth I died, there were already 32 colleges in existence.

Although popular opinion tends to link the two universities, they have widely divergent backgrounds, allegiances, traditions and atmospheres. It goes much deeper than the largely sentimental division into Light and Dark Blue, which occurs annually on the occasion of what is now a national sporting event, the Boat Race.

This fine book of photographs by R.S. Magowan reveals the similarities and contrasts between these two celebrated university towns. Special attention in naturally paid to the buildings and grounds of the famous colleges, but space has also been found for other landmarks and monuments as well as for the undergraduates themselves, both in sober and frivolous mood.

Mr Raymond Postgate, who has the unusual experience of having lived and been educated in both cities, has contributed a wise and affectionate introduction to the book, noting, a little wistfully, some of the changes which have inevitably occurred since the days when horsedrawn trams rumbled through Cambridge and motor-cars had not begun to choke Oxford. But it is the measure of Oxford and Cambridge's strength that time cannot rob them either of their separate identities or of their joint and unique significance.

Other books in this series

Each volume in this series is a singular portrait of a city or pair of cities by photographers well known in the field. The result in each instance is a unity of approach which will surprise and delight those already familiar with these cities and who wish to possess a memorable and permanent record of them; and for those who wish to know the famous cities better, these books will prove an invaluable aid.

Each book has a specially written introduction contributed by a distinguished personality associated with the city or cities concerned.

Titles still available

LONDON
(A. P. Herbert)

ROME
(Richard Aldington)

New titles

DUBLIN AND CORK
(Kate O'Brien)

VENICE
(Michael Redgrave)

Trinity Hall, Cambridge

OXFORD &
CAMBRIDGE

A Book of Photographs by

R. S. MAGOWAN

With an introduction by

RAYMOND POSTGATE

SPRING BOOKS · LONDON

Published by

SPRING BOOKS

SPRING HOUSE • SPRING PLACE • LONDON N W 5

© Books for Pleasure Ltd 1961

Printed in Czechoslovakia

T 816

Contents

FORTIS EST VERITAS

THE ARMS OF THE CITY OF OXFORD
LES ARMES DE LA CITÉ D'OXFORD
WAPPEN DER STADT OXFORD

Introduction

WHEN I was small, I remember, the world was divided into two kinds of people, Dark Blues and Light Blues. Oxford or Cambridge; you had to be one or the other. (Not 'for' one or the other; you never said 'Are you for Oxford?' but always 'Are you Oxford?' — or Cambridge). Even now, one day in the year, England remembers that division and on Boat Race Day everyone is either Dark Blue or Light Blue. But I am both, and always must be both. For I was born in Cambridge and lived there, a Light Blue, till I was twelve; but I went to Oxford as my university. So I cannot choose between them; both are my *almae matres*.

The Cambridge which I saw first, and which I still see hidden behind — not much hidden, either — the present Cambridge was an older town than the Oxford. It was the Cambridge of horsedrawn trams, of muffin men ringing their bells at nightfall, of Coe Fen still wild, with no great road running across it. The water ran sluggishly through it; water beetles danced endlessly in the sun on the river's surface; a child could lose himself quietly there a whole day through. The horse trams ran from the railway station to the market place — 'ran'? Hardly the word; the one horse walked scarcely faster than a man would, but assuredly faster than the old ladies who mostly used the service. Even for them the speed was so sedate that one standing on the kerb could still finish her conversation with one on the departing tram's platform. My mother once heard the most sinister of these last sentences: 'But it was the buttonhook that opened his eyes', squealed the old lady. But, in the tempo of those times, the traffic was already dangerous; on my bicycle I was run down, and might have been killed, by a hansom cab.

Oxford was more like it is today, except that it was quieter; the motor buses were there, but the motor car was rare and the motor lorry rarer. But the two cities showed then, as these pictures show still, their essential difference, as well as their essential similarities. Summarised in a few words, the truth is this: Oxford is more beautiful piece by piece. Cambridge is more beautiful as a whole.

Oxford you can see from afar — from Boar's Hill — spread out with a forest of spires; Cambridge you must enter to appreciate; from a distance it is a confusion of spilt roofs. Also, and by the way, Oxford is Tory, Cambridge is Whig.

There are more similarities than differences, of course, as there must be with two ancient university cities, both packed with old buildings, both on a river, both built on what is nearly a marsh, and both with a large population of dons and students. But their variation one from another is more interesting to the foreign observer.

Cambridge is in essence still a market town; it has a unity which Oxford doesn't have. The grand buildings are integrated with it; the narrow medievally-planned streets assimilate them as part of their own pattern. The town of Cambridge is interesting in itself; it is not just an appendage of the University. Market Hill — which is a flat square into which narrow streets run at each corner — has a life of its own every market day; it is a county-town market in its own right. Cambridge streets are overcrowded, true, as almost all county-town streets are, but they are overcrowded by the natural exuberances of a university-plus-county town — too many dons, students, motor bicycles and bicycles and too many farmers, lorries and traders bringing in or taking out their goods. But Oxford, which has no centre of old county-town life like Market Hill, is overcrowded and over-noised (if that is a word) by an external and alien plague. It is oppressed and elbowed by a monster, a Beast crouching next to it. Follow the unending, noisy, sluggishly-choked traffic down High Street to Magdalen bridge, cross it, and then you will see three roads spreading out like a fan. They lead to the great new, tedious modern suburb of Cowley, which has been swelling ever since Mr Morris started making his cars there, and whose inhabitants, vehicles and trucks pour into Oxford, destroying its quiet, shaking its buildings and making its streets impassable.

There are, probably, no finer buildings set all in a group than the Cambridge Colleges which back upon the river. Nowhere, surely, can there be a more delightful walk than along 'the Backs'. There are trees on the far side, keeping the 'stockbroker's Tudor' houses away, there is the smooth slow river, there is the series of bridges across to the gardens of the various colleges, running down green to the water, there are the college buildings themselves. As you walk along, or punt along on the river, there is a sequence of beauty: Peterhouse, Queens', St Catherines, King's, Clare, Trinity Hall, Trinity, St John's.

But I will maintain that there are individual colleges in Oxford which are finer than anything you can find in Cambridge. Magdalen College, for example: the tower that rises at the foot of High Street, near to the bridge, is the most graceful of all the academic buildings there are, no matter where you view it from; and all Magdalen College buildings are equally perfect of their kind, harmonising even though they are of different centuries. The tower is Gothic; there is a classical court from which you can watch deer feeding in the paddock, and out of which you can walk for a tramp round meadows which have no equivalent in Cambridge.

Perhaps it is a biased love for my old college which makes me add that there is no view in Cambridge like that of the low grey line of the second quad in St John's, seen from the far end of the vast impeccable lawn, and covered in purple wistaria.

There are, undoubtedly, some particular buildings in Cambridge that arrest your eyes and may even catch your breath. The Great Gate of Trinity is among them. It owes something to the cunning use of colour on stone. Your eyes are caught by the bright escutcheons of the founders, but most of all by the one that is blank, belonging to the baby who died young.

Demortuus infans, it says beneath it: 'died an infant'. Not just 'died', in fact, *mortuus*, but *demortuus*, 'died off', 'quite dead' — there is something pathetic about that strained Latin word.

There are several things that both cities have in common and which no improvements are likely to deprive them of. One is space. You can still walk into the great court of Trinity in Cambridge, or Tom quad at Christ Church in Oxford, and find yourself in the middle of a vast rectangular area, kept such for no better reason than that symmetry and civilisation call for it. You may calculate, if it pleases you, how many tiny three-roomed flats or offices in 16-storied concrete blocks could be run up in this space by commercial architects if they were allowed, and you may even rejoice in the thought that they never will be allowed.

The cities have in common, too, their slow smooth rivers, where young men and women push about in punts, the least convenient or sensible means of river locomotion. If you are a male, the punt pole pours water up your sleeve, and if you hold on to it you will be left clinging to it like a monkey on a stick while the punt smoothly slides away. If you are female, it will cause you to stick out your behind in a manner that even the most besotted lover cannot call glamorous. But the youth of both sexes, in both cities, delight in it, and if the sight of them is absurd it is also charming. Young men racing, too, in those long thin boats, in the May races in Cambridge and the Eights week in Oxford, who could fail to be delighted by them?

But the two cities are not just a playground for youth. Youth itself, as it pours out of lectures or stands round examination halls, in subfusc garments and candid ties ('dark' and 'white' in more ordinary language), bears witness to this. Oxford and Cambridge are centres of learning and of civilisation; their elders, the dons themselves, more exactly personify the spirit of the cities, 'regal dons', in Belloc's lines, who

> '... sail in amply billowing gowns
> Enormous through the sacred town,
> Bearing from College to their homes
> Deep cargoes of gigantic tomes.'

Introduction

QUAND j'étais petit, je me souviens, le monde se divisait en deux catégories: les bleus marine et les bleus ciel. Oxford ou Cambridge; il fallait être l'un ou l'autre (non pas pour l'un ou pour l'autre; on ne disait jamais «Etes-vous pour Oxford?» mais «Etes-vous Oxford?» — ou Cambridge). Même aujourd'hui, cette distinction revit chez nous une fois l'an, le jour de la fameuse course d'aviron, où chacun est soit bleu marine, soit bleu ciel. Pour moi, je suis l'un et l'autre, et le resterai toujours, car si je suis né à Cambridge et y ai vécu, bleu ciel, jusqu'à l'âge de douze ans, j'ai ensuite été étudiant à l'Université d'Oxford. Je ne saurais donc choisir entre les deux rivales, qui sont l'une et l'autre mes *almae matres*.

La Cambridge que j'ai d'abord connue, et que je retrouve cachée — mal cachée à vrai dire — derrière la Cambridge d'aujourd'hui, était une ville plus ancienne qu'Oxford. C'était la Cambridge des tramways à chevaux, des marchands de «muffins» faisant tinter leurs cloches à la tombée du jour, de Coe Fen sauvage encore, sans la grande route qui la traverse aujourd'hui. La rivière coulait paresseusement; les dytiques dansaient sans fin dans le soleil à la surface de l'eau; un enfant pouvait se perdre là tranquillement toute une journée. Les omnibus allaient de la gare à la place du marché; le cheval unique marchait à peine plus vite qu'un homme à pied, mais sûrement plus vite que les vieilles dames usagères du service. Même pour elles, la vitesse était si «confortable» que l'une, debout au bord du trottoir, pouvait encore achever sa conversation avec sa compagne, déjà montée sur la plate-forme. Ma mère entendit ainsi un jour de la bouche d'une de ces respectables dames ce dernier mot vraiment sinistre: «Mais ce fut le tire-bouton qui lui ouvrit les yeux!» Même au rythme d'alors, la rue était déjà dangereuse; je me souviens d'avoir été renversé, à bicyclette, par un «cab», et j'ai bien failli ne pas en réchapper.

Oxford ressemblait davantage à la ville d'aujourd'hui, si ce n'est qu'elle était plus calme. Il y avait des omnibus à moteur, mais les automobiles étaient rares et les camions plus rares encore. Pourtant on distinguait déjà entre les deux villes, comme ces images le montrent, des différences et des analogies fondamentales. En un mot, elles se résument à ceci: Oxford est plus belle pièce à pièce — Cambridge l'est davantage comme ensemble.

On peut voir Oxford de loin, de Boar's Hill, hérissée de cent clochers. Cambridge, il faut y entrer pour la connaître; de loin, ce n'est qu'un fouillis de toits épars. Aussi, soit dit en passant, Oxford est tory, alors que Cambridge est whig.

Il y a plus d'analogies que de différences, certes, et cela est naturel puisqu'il s'agit de deux anciennes villes universitaires, riches en vieilles pierres, bâties au bord d'une rivière sur ce qui est presque un marais, et comptant toutes deux une vaste population d'étudiants et de professeurs. Mais ce sont les contrastes qui frappent davantage le visiteur étranger.

Cambridge est encore essentiellement un bourg; elle a une unité que l'on ne retrouve pas à Oxford. Les grands édifices se sont fondus dans la ville, et côtoient sans heurts les étroites ruelles du Moyen Age. La ville de Cambridge est intéressante en elle-même; ce n'est pas uniquement une dépendance de l'Université. Market Hill, place parfaitement plane malgré son nom, aux quatre coins de laquelle débouchent des rues étroites, a une vie qui lui est tout à fait propre les jours de foire; c'est à lui seul un vrai bourg de campagne. Les rues de Cambridge sont surpeuplées, il est vrai, comme celle de tous les chefs-lieux de comté, mais elles sont surpeuplées par les exhubérances naturelles d'une ville qui est à la fois centre universitaire et administratif: trop de maîtres et d'élèves, de motos et de bicyclettes, trop de paysans, de camions et de marchands apportant ou enlevant leurs marchandises. Oxford au contraire, qui n'a pas de «bourg» comme Market Hill, est surpeuplée et «surbruitée», si le mot existe, par un fléau extérieur et étranger. Elle est bousculée, tyrannisée par un monstre, un fauve accroupi à ses flancs. Suivez l'interminable file des véhicules qui serpentent roue à roue le long de High Street jusqu'à Magdalen Bridge, passez le pont: vous verrez trois routes qui s'écartent en patte d'oie. Elles mènent au grand et terne faubourg moderne de Cowley qui n'a cessé de s'étendre depuis que Morris commença d'y fabriquer ses automobiles et dont les habitants, les camions, les voitures convergent vers Oxford, détruisant son calme, faisant trembler ses murs et engorgeant ses rues.

Il n'y a probablement pas d'ensemble architectural plus réussi que les façades des collèges de Cambridge qui donnent, côté cour, sur la rivière. Il n'est sans doute nulle part de promenade plus délicieuse qu'au long de ce qu'on appelle les «backs». Au loin des rangées d'arbres, qui cachent les maisons «faux Tudor» de la bourgeoisie locale, puis voici la rivière majestueuse et lente, une série de ponts qui mènent aux jardins des divers collèges, tapis de verdure au bord de l'eau; enfin les collèges eux-mêmes. A la vue du promeneur, ou du rameur, s'offrent ces joyaux d'un autre âge: Peterhouse, Queens', Ste Catherine, King's, Clare, Trinity Hall, Trinity, St John's.

Mais je prétends qu'il existe à Oxford des collèges plus beaux encore que ceux-là. Magdalen College, par example: la tour qui s'élève au pied de High Street, près du pont, est la plus gracieuse de toutes les maisons d'université, d'où que vous la regardiez; et tous les édifices qui composent Magdalen College sont également parfaits dans leur genre, malgré leur diversité de style. La tour est gothique; il y a une cour d'ordonnance classique d'où l'on peut voir des daims brouter dans un parc et d'où l'on peut partir pour une promenade à travers prés qui n'a pas d'égal à Cambridge.

Peut-être est-ce un préjugé en faveur de mon ancien collège qui me fait dire ici qu'il n'y a rien à Cambridge d'aussi beau que la basse silhouette grise du deuxième «quad» de St John's, couverte de glycines mauves, vue du bout de la vaste et impeccable pelouse qui lui fait face.

Certes, il y a certains édifices à Cambridge qui retiennent l'oeil et même arrêtent le souffle. La grande porte de Trinity, par exemple. Elle doit beaucoup à l'emploi ingénieux de la couleur sur la pierre. L'oeil est séduit par les brillants écussons des fondateurs et surtout par l'écusson blanc, celui de l'enfant qui mourut très jeune: «*Demortuus infans*», dit l'inscription: «mort enfant». Plus que mort, au demeurant, non seulement «*mortuus*» mais «*demortuus*»: «arraché à la vie»; je vois quelque chose de pathétique dans ce mot latin renforcé.

Il y a plusieurs choses que les deux cités ont en commun et qu'aucun embellissement ne pourra jamais leur enlever. L'une est l'espace: vous pouvez encore vous promener dans la grande cour de Trinity à Cambridge, ou dans Tom Quad à Christ Church d'Oxford, et vous trouver au milieu d'une vaste étendue rectangulaire, ainsi conservée pour une simple raison de symétrie et parce que la civilisation le veut ainsi. Vous pouvez calculer, si telle est votre fantaisie, combien de petits appartements de trois pièces ou de grands immeubles de 16 étages l'on pourrait bâtir en cet endroit si la permission en était donnée, et vous pouvez vous réjouir de savoir que ce ne sera jamais autorisé.

Les deux villes ont aussi en commun leurs douces rivières, où les jeunes gens se promènent en barques plates, moyen de locomotion des plus incommodes et des plus illogiques sur une surface d'eau. Si vous êtes un garçon, la perche laisse égoutter un filet d'eau qui détrempe vos manches et si vous vous tenez trop fort à la perche, vous vous retrouvez accroché désespérément à elle comme un singe au bout d'une branche tandis que la barque se dérobe doucement sous vos pieds. Si vous êtes une fille, vous vous tiendrez assise en cambrant les reins d'une manière que même l'amant le plus aveugle ne saurait appeler élégante. Mais les jeunes adorent cet exercice, et s'ils paraissent un peu ridicules, ils n'en sont pas moins charmants. Les jeunes sportifs aussi, qui s'affrontent dans de longs canots effilés, lors des courses de mai à Cambridge, ou de la semaine des Huit à Oxford, qui peut s'empêcher de les admirer?

Mais les deux villes ne sont pas seulement un terrain de récréation. Les jeunes eux-mêmes, qu'on voit sortir de leurs cours ou s'assembler près de leurs collèges, en vêtements sombres et en cravates claires («dark» et «white» en langage ordinaire) en portent témoignage. Oxford et Cambridge sont des foyers de culture et de civilisation; leurs aînés, les professeurs, incarnent exactement l'esprit des deux villes, royaux personnages qui, suivant les termes d'Hilaire Belloc,

> « . . . naviguent dans leurs amples robes,
> Enormes par la ville sacrée,
> Portant du collège à leur home,
> Des cargaisons d'immenses tomes.»

Einleitung

Als ich noch ein kleiner Junge war, bestand die Welt fein säuberlich geschieden aus zwei Arten Menschen, Dunkelblauen und Hellblauen, oder Menschen aus Oxford und Menschen aus Cambridge. Oxford oder Cambridge, das eine oder das andere, und sonst gab es nichts. Man war auch nicht etwa „für Oxford" oder „für Cambridge", sondern man „war Oxford", oder man „war Cambridge", dunkelblau oder hellblau, und an einem Tag im Jahr ist auch heute noch ganz England dunkelblau oder hellblau, nämlich am Boat Race Day, dem Tag der großen Ruderregatta zwischen den beiden Universitäten. Aber ich bin ein besonderer Fall, denn ich bin jetzt beides, dunkelblau und hellblau, und muß es bleiben bis ans Ende meiner Tage. Und das kommt daher, daß ich in Cambridge geboren wurde und aufwuchs, aber dann nach Oxford auf die Universität ging. Mir ist es also verwehrt, zwischen ihnen zu wählen, denn sie sind beide meine *almae matres*.

Das Cambridge, das ich als kleiner Junge kannte und das sich für mich immer doch hinter dem heutigen Cambridge verbirgt, bot ein älteres Stadtbild als Oxford. In dem Cambridge meiner Jugend gab es noch Pferdebahnen, Semmelverkäufer läuteten ihre Schellen an Winterabenden von den Straßenecken, und Coe Fen war ein wildes, weltentrücktes Stück Land, durch das es keine Straße gab. Nur der Fluß, die Cam, wälzte sich träge und schwerfällig hindurch, und Wasserkäfer tanzten ohne Unterlaß über seine Oberfläche hin; es war ein Kinderparadies, in dem man stunden- und stundenlang dem Rest der Welt Adieu sagen konnte. Die Pferdebahn fuhr vom Bahnhof zum Marktplatz; aber „fuhr" ist etwas übertrieben gesagt, denn das von einem Gaul gezogene Gefährt kam kaum schneller voran als ein Mann in gewöhnlichem Fußgängerschritt. Immerhin, für ältere Damen war es die gegebene Transportgelegenheit; aber selbst für sie ging alles so gemütlich ab, daß eine an der Haltestelle zurückbleibende Dame ihre Unterhaltung mit einer auf der Plattform der abfahrenden Straßenbahn stehenden Freundin in aller Ruhe beenden konnte. An modernen Maßstäben gemessen war also der Verkehr weder stark noch schnell; aber trotzdem war er auch nicht ganz ungefährlich. Als Radfahrer wurde ich einmal von einer Droschke überfahren und kam eben noch mit dem Leben davon.

Oxford sah zu meiner Studentenzeit nicht viel anders aus als heute; nur ruhiger war es natürlich. Es gab zwar schon Autobusse, aber nur sehr wenige Autos und noch weniger Lastwagen. Damals schon zeigten mir die beiden Städte, genau wie die in diesem Bande gesammelten Bilder es heute noch tun, ihre wesentlichen Unterschiede und ihre wesentlichen Ähnlichkeiten. In ein paar Worten zusammengefaßt, könnte man es so sagen, daß in Einzelheiten Oxford, aber als Ganzes gesehen Cambridge schöner ist. Schaut man von Boar's Hill auf Oxford hinunter, so liegt es vor einem ausgebreitet wie ein Wald von Türmen. Aber um zu sehen, was Cambridge zu bieten hat, muß man mitten in der Stadt sein, denn von fern sieht es nur aus wie ein wirres Durcheinander von Dächern. Und noch ein Unterschied: Oxford, so heißt es allgemein, ist *Tory*, konservativ, und Cambridge ist *Whig*, liberal.

Natürlich sind die Ähnlichkeiten zahlreicher als die Unterschiede, wie sich das ja bei zwei altehrwürdigen Universitätsstädten versteht, die beide voll alter Baulichkeiten sind, beide an einem Fluß liegen, beide auf sumpfähnlichem Gelände errichtet wurden und beide einen Großteil ihrer Einwohnerschaft ihren Universitäten verdanken. Aber die Unterschiede sind dem Fremden wohl interessanter als die Ähnlichkeiten.

Cambridge ist heute immer noch dem Wesen nach die „market town", die Kreisstadt mit Marktrecht, und als solche besitzt es eine Einheitlichkeit, die Oxford nicht kennt. Seine großen Gebäude fügen sich den engen, mittelalterlichen Straßen als selbstverständlicher Teil des Stadtplans ein. Allein als Stadt schon kann Cambridge Interesse beanspruchen, denn es ist mehr als nur ein Anhängsel der Universität. Market Hill, ein flacher Platz mit Einmündungen enger Straßen an allen Ecken, ist an jedem Markttag voll überschäumenden Lebens und beweist einem ohne weiteres, daß die Stadt das Markt- und Geschäftszentrum ihres Kreises ist. Die Straßen sind überfüllt, wie die Straßen aller Kreisstädte an Markttagen überfüllt sind; aber hier in dieser Kreisstadt kommt noch das Universitätselement hinzu, und daher sind die Straßen übervoll nicht nur von zu viel Bauern, zu viel Lieferwagen und zu viel Hausfrauen, sondern auch von zu viel Dozenten und zu viel Studenten und zu viel Motorrädern und zu viel Fahrrädern. Oxford hingegen hat keinen Market Hill, keinen Mittelpunkt eines traditionellen Kreisstadtlebens, und sein Lärm und seine Überfüllung rührten von etwas ganz anderem her. Oxford lebt sozusagen im Schatten eines Ungeheuers, einer ganz fremdartigen Plage. Wenn man der endlosen, lärmerfüllten, verkehrsverstopften High Street, der Hauptstraße, zur Magdalen Bridge folgt und über die Brücke geht, sieht man sich drei fächerartig ausstrahlenden Straßen gegenüber. Sie alle führen in die große, neue, langweiligmoderne Vorstadt Cowley, die gewachsen ist und wächst und weiterwächst, seit Mr Morris anfing, hier seine berühmten Autos zu fabrizieren, und es sind die Tausende und Tausende aus Cowley und ihre Last- und Lieferwagen, die Oxford bis zum Rand füllen, seine Ruhe zerstören, seine Gebäude bis auf die Grundfesten erschüttern und seine Straßen unpassierbar machen.

Ich glaube nicht, daß, als Ganzes betrachtet, es eine schönere Gruppe von Gebäuden gibt als die *Colleges* in Cambridge, deren Gärten und Rasen auf der Rückseite ans Ufer der Cam grenzen — und hier muß ich erklärend einschalten, daß *Colleges* in Oxford und Cambridge finanziell unabhängige Studiengemeinschaften von Gelehrten und Studenten sind, die den Großteil des Lehrkörpers und der Studentenschaft der Universität umfassen. Nun, ich kann mir keinen schöneren Spaziergang vorstellen als *The Backs* entlang, wie der Teil von Cambridge zwischen dem Fluß und den *Colleges* genannt wird. Auf der anderen Seite der Cam stehen hochgewachsene Bäume, die die nicht immer geschmackvollen Häuser der Neureichen dem Blick entziehen, langsam gleitet die Cam dahin, über die sich eine Reihe von Brücken in die Gärten der verschiedenen *Colleges* schwingt, und dahinter ragen deren Gebäude selbst auf, in ihrer Schönheit wie Perlen an einer Kette einander folgend: Peterhouse, Queens', St Catherine's, King's, Clare, Trinity Hall, Trinity und St John's College.

Meiner Meinung nach aber gibt es einzelne *Colleges* in Oxford, die schöner sind als die schönsten in Cambridge. Der Turm von Magdalen College am Ende der High Street bei der Brücke ist das anmutigste Universitätsgebäude, das man sich vorstellen kann, von welcher Seite aus man es auch sieht, und die ganzen übrigen Baulichkeiten von Magdalen College erreichen denselben Grad von Vollkommenheit, eine wundervolle Harmonie aus Stein, obwohl ihre einzelnen Bestandteile aus ganz verschiedenen Perioden stammen. Der Turm selbst ist gotisch; dahinter dehnt sich ein Hof in klassischem Stil, von dem aus man Rotwild im Gehege grasen sehen und dann über weite Wiesen wandern kann, eine Kombination, die es in Cambridge einfach nicht gibt. Mein altes *College* war St John's, und man wird mir ein gewisses Vorurteil zugute halten müssen, wenn ich sage, daß man ein Bild wie das der niedrigen grauen, von purpurroten Glyzinen überwachsenen Fassade des zweiten Gebäudehofes von St John's, von der anderen Seite der weiten wundervollen Rasenfläche her gesehen, in Cambridge vergeblich suchen wird.

Zweifellos gibt es auch in Cambridge Bauten, an denen man nicht teilnahmslos vorbeigehen kann, die sogar überwältigend wirken können. Eines von ihnen ist *The Great Gate of Trinity*, das große Tor von Trinity, vielleicht weil verschiedenfarbige Steinarten in seinem Mauerwerk überaus geschickt verwendet worden sind. Es trägt die Wappenschilder der Gründer von Trinity, und unter ihnen entdeckt man erstaunlicherweise ein Schild, auf dem das Wappen fehlt. Es gehört einem kleinen Kinde aus der Gründerfamilie, das in frühster Jugend starb. „*Demortuus infans*" heißt es darunter, „verstarb als Kind", nicht einfach „starb", *mortuus*, sondern *demortuus*, „verstarb", mit einem etwas pathetischen Beiklang.

Ein paar Vorzüge haben beide Städte gemein, die ihnen wohl keine Entwicklung der Zukunft rauben wird. Einer davon ist Raum, weiter freier Raum. Wie früher, so kann man auch heute noch in den großen Hof von Trinity in Cambridge oder den *Tom Quad* genannten Gebäudehof in Christ Church in Oxford wandern und sich auf einmal auf einer weiten rechteckigen Fläche finden, deren einziger Existenzgrund der ist, daß die Gesetze der Symmetrie und einer feinfühligen Lebenskunst danach verlangten. Manch einer mag vielleicht Vergnügen an der Berechnung finden, wie viele Dreizimmerwohnungen oder sechzehnstöckige Bürogebäude hier errichtet werden könnten, wenn es je erlaubt würde — und manch anderer ein vielleicht noch größeres Vergnügen an der Tatsache, daß es nie erlaubt werden wird.

Gemeinsam sind beiden Städten ferner ihre trägen kleinen Flüsse, auf denen die Jugend beiderlei Geschlechts in Punts, flachen Booten, spazierenfährt. Mit diesen ruderlosen Flachbooten, die nur eine lange Stange haben, mit der man sich vorwärtsstoßen muß, umgehen zu können ist eine Kunst, bei der die meisten

Jünglinge sich naß und junge Mädchen sich lächerlich machen. Trotzdem ist es der Lieblingszeitvertreib der akademischen Jugend. Und wessen Herz würde nicht schneller schlagen, wenn er die jungen Universitäts-athleten in ihren langen schmalen Ruderbooten in der Mairegatta in Cambridge oder der Woche der Achter-rennen in Oxford dahinschießen sieht!

Wenn man nun aber glaubt, daß Oxford und Cambridge nichts als Spielplätze für Studenten sind, hat man sich sehr geirrt. Man braucht sie nur zu sehen, wie sie aus den Vorlesungen herausströmen oder in dunklen Gewändern um die Prüfungssäle herumstehen, um sich von der Wirklichkeit des Universitätslebens zu über-zeugen. Oxford und Cambridge sind Mittelpunkte der Gelehrsamkeit und der Kultur, und ihr Geist verkörpert sich vielleicht am treffendsten in ihren Professoren und Dozenten, den „königlichen Dons", wenn sie, frei nach den Versen des englischen Dichters Belloc,

„ . . . segeln in wehendem Talar
Majestätisch vom College Jahr um Jahr
Durch die Stadt, die sie verzaubert hält,
Beladen mit dem Geist der Welt."

THE ARMS OF THE CITY OF CAMBRIDGE
LES ARMES DE LA CITÉ DE CAMBRIDGE
WAPPEN DER STADT CAMBRIDGE

13

Index

OXFORD

CAMBRIDGE

COLOUR PLATES

All Souls, Oxford

The Backs, Cambridge

Magdalen, Oxford

OXFORD

Magdalen: porter's lodge
Magdalen: la loge du portier
Magdalen: Pförtnerhaus

Magdalen: the Cloisters, with carved figures on buttresses
Magdalen: le cloître, aux contreforts ornés de sculptures
Magdalen: der Kreuzgang mit gemeißelten Figuren auf den Strebepfeilern

William of Wayneflete, Bishop of Winchester and Lord High Chancellor, founded Magdalen in 1458
Magdalen fut fondé en 1458 par William of Wayneflete, évêque de Winchester et Lord Grand Chancelier
William von Wayneflete, Bischof von Winchester und Großkanzler von England, gründete Magdalen College im Jahre 1458

Magdalen: punting on the Cherwell
Magdalen: en barque sur le Cherwell
Magdalen: Flachboote auf der Cherwell

Magdalen: First Quad, dating from 1475
Magdalen: First Quad, qui date de 1475
Magdalen: der Erste Gebäudehof, 1475 entstanden

Magdalen Tower and boys of Magdalen College School
La tour de Magdalen et les écoliers de Magdalen College School
Der Turm von Magdalen College und Schüler der Magdalen-
College-Schule

New Buildings at Magdalen, dating from 1733
Les nouveaux bâtiments de Magdalen, qui datent de 1733
Neuere, 1733 entstandene Teile von Magdalen College

23

Christ Church. Wolsey conceived the plan for his 'Cardinal's College' in 1525
Christ Church. Wolsey conçut le plan de son «Collège du Cardinal» en 1525
Christ Church. Wolsey faßte den Plan zu seinem „Kardinals-College" im Jahre 1525

Christ Church: Tom Tower, designed by Wren. The seven-ton bell is called Great Tom
Christ Church: Tom Tower, oeuvre de Wren. La cloche, qui pèse sept tonnes, porte le surnom de Great Tom
Christ Church: „Tom Tower", nach dem Entwurf von Wren erbaut. Die sieben Tonnen schwere Glocke heißt „Great Tom"

Christ Church: Cathedral Buildings, from the Broadwalk
Christ Church: les bâtiments de la cathédrale, vu de Broadwalk
Christ Church: Gebäude der Kathedrale, vom Broadwalk aus gesehen

Christ Church: fan-vaulting in the Hall, possibly the finest in Oxford. Henry VIII and Charles I both banqueted here
Voûtes en éventail à Christ Church Hall, peut-être le plus beau d'Oxford. Henri VIII et Charles 1er y tinrent banquet
Christ Church: Fächergewölbe in der Hall (Speisesaal), möglicherweise der schönsten in Oxford. Heinrich VIII. und Karl I. tafelten hier

The figure of Mercury adorns the fountain in the centre of Tom Quad
La statue de Mercure orne la fontaine qui s'élève au centre de Tom Quad
Das Standbild Merkurs ziert den Springbrunnen in der Mitte von „Tom Quad"

Christ Church's Tom Quad, about 100 yards square, is the largest of all Oxford quadrangles

Christ Church: Tom Quad, avec près de 100 mètres de côté, est la plus grande cour carrée d'Oxford

„Tom Quad" in Christ Church mit seinen 100 Metern im Quadrat ist der größte Hof in Oxford

All Souls: the twin towers dominating the quadrangle built by Nicholas Hawksmoor
All Souls: les deux tours jumelles dominant la cour carrée bâtie par Nicolas Hawksmoor
All Souls: die Zwillingstürme beherrschen den Collegehof, den Nicholas Hawksmoor errichtete

All Souls is unique in that it has never admitted undergraduates
All Souls a cette particularité de n'avoir jamais admis d'étudiants au dessous du niveau de la licence
All Souls steht einzig darin da, daß es keine Studenten aufnimmt, sondern nur bereits Promovierte

New College: the Front Quad
New College: Front Quad
New College: der Vordere Collegehof

New College: bicycle repairs
New College: réparation de bicyclette
New College: beim Fahrradreparieren

All Souls: the Cloisters and entrance gateway,
dwarfed by the Radcliffe Camera

All Souls: le cloître et la porte d'entrée, devant
la coupole de Radcliffe Camera

All Souls: der Kreuzgang und das Eingangstor,
überragt von Radcliffe Camera

The gardens of New College with part of the 13th century city wall. The college was founded in 1379 by William of Wykeham, Bishop of Winchester and Lord High Chancellor

Les jardins de New College, avec une partie de l'enceinte du XIIIe siècle. Le collège fut fondé en 1379 par William de Wykeham, évêque de Winchester et Lord Grand Chancelier

Gartenanlagen von New College mit einem Teil der Stadtmauer aus dem 13. Jahrhundert. William von Wykeham, Bischof von Winchester und Großkanzler, gründete New College im Jahre 1379

New College gardens and Thomas Robinson's wrought-iron gate. These buildings date from the 17th and 18th centuries, but the Muniment Tower on the left was constructed in 1380

Les jardins de New College et la grille en fer forgé de Thomas Robinson. Ces bâtiments datent des XVIIe et XVIIIe siècles, mais la Tour Muniment, sur la gauche, a été construite en 1380

New College: Gartenanlagen und das von Thomas Robinson geschaffene schmiedeeiserne Tor. Die Gebäude stammen aus dem 17. und 18. Jahrhundert; nur der „Muniment Tower", links, wurde 1380 erbaut

The High Street gate-house of Brasenose College, founded in 1509. Its name derives from a brass door-knocker in the shape of a lion's head, now in the Hall

La loge de Brasenose College, High Street. Ce collège, fondé en 1509, tire son nom (nez de cuivre) d'un heurtoir de cuivre en forme de tête de lion, que l'on voit encore dans le Hall

Der Eingang des 1509 gegründeten Brasenose College an der High Street. Sein Name über Brassnose-Messignase wird von einem wie ein Löwenkopf geformten Türklopfer aus Messing abgeleitet, der sich jetzt in der Hall befindet

Brasenose: the late 19th century High Street front
Brasenose: la façade sur High Street, fin XIXᵉ siècle
Brasenose: die Fassade zur High Street, aus dem späten 19. Jahrhundert

The 16th century quadrangle of Brasenose
La cour carrée de Brasenose, qui date du XVIᵉ siècle
Brasenose: der Collegehof aus dem 16. Jahrhundert

Balliol: chess in the First Quad
Balliol: partie d'échecs à First Quad
Balliol: Schach im Ersten Gebäudehof

Balliol: croquet in front of the Hall
Balliol: partie de croquet devant le Hall
Balliol: Krocket vor der Hall

Exeter College was founded in 1314 by Walter de Stapledon, Bishop of Exeter. Most of the buildings are Victorian

Exeter College fut fondé en 1314 par Walter de Stapledon, évêque d'Exeter. Les bâtiments sont pour le plupart de l'époque victorienne

Exeter College wurde 1314 von Walter von Stapledon, Bischof von Exeter, gegründet. Die meisten Gebäude stammen aus der Zeit der Königin Viktoria

Balliol is one of the earliest colleges, founded in 1263–1267 by John Balliol and his wife, parents of John Balliol, King of Scots

Balliol est l'un des plus anciens collèges. Il fut fondé entre 1263 et 1267 par John Balliol et sa femme, parents de John Balliol, roi d'Ecosse

Balliol ist eines der ältesten Colleges; es stammt aus den Jahren 1263 bis 1267 und wurde von John Balliol und seiner Frau, den Eltern des Schottenkönigs John Balliol, gegründet

Oriel: the 17th century Hall, with statues of the Virgin and Child, Edward II and James I. Edward II and his chaplain, Adam de Brome, founded the college in 1326

Oriel: le Hall, construit au XVIIe siècle, est orné de statues de la Vierge à l'enfant, d'Edouard II et de Jacques 1er. Edouard II et son chapelain, Adam de Brome, fondèrent le collège en 1326

Oriel: die Hall aus dem 17. Jahrhundert mit Statuen der Mutter Gottes mit dem Jesuskind und der Könige Eduard II. und Jakob I. Eduard II. und sein Hausprediger Adam von Brome gründeten Oriel College im Jahre 1326

Corpus Christi: Front Quad, with the sundial surmounted by a pelican, the college emblem. Smallest of Oxford colleges, it was founded in 1516 by Richard Foxe, Bishop of Winchester

Corpus Christi: Front Quad, avec son cadran solaire surmonté d'un pélican, emblème du collège. Fondé par Richard Foxe, évêque de Winchester, en 1516, Corpus Christi est le plus petit collège d'Oxford

Corpus Christi: der Vordere Collegehof mit der Sonnenuhr, auf dem das Collegewahrzeichen, ein Pelikan, sitzt. Das College, in 1516 von Richard Foxe, Bischof von Winchester, gegründet, ist das kleinste in Oxford

Thomas Tindall was the founder of Pembroke in 1624, and Samuel Johnson studied here for 14 months
C'est Thomas Tindall qui fonda Pembroke en 1624. Samuel Johnson y fut étudiant pendant 14 mois
Thomas Tindall gründete Pembroke College im Jahre 1624, und Samuel Johnson war 14 Monate hier Student

The gardens and Chapel of Wadham College, founded in 1610 by Nicholas Wadham, and completed after his death by his widow
Les jardins et la chapelle de Wadham College, fondé en 1610 par Nicolas Wadham et achevé après sa mort par sa veuve
Gärten und Kapelle von Wadham College. Nicholas Wadham gründete es 1610, und nach seinem Tode vollendete seine Witwe den Bau

Wadham College Hall is the third largest in Oxford and
has a fine hammer-beam roof

Wadham College Hall est l'un des trois plus grands halls
d'Oxford. Il est fameux pour son très beau toit

Die Hall von Wadham College ist die drittgrößte in
Oxford und hat ein schönes Stichbalkendach

Wadham College Chapel has a fine East window. It is the only
college which is virtually unaltered since its foundation

Wadham College Chapel, dont on admire le beau vitrail est.
Wadham est le seul collège resté pratiquement intact depuis
sa fondation

Die Kapelle von Wadham College hat ein sehr schönes Ostfenster. Wadham ist das einzige College, das seit seiner Er-
bauung fast unverändert geblieben ist

St Edmund Hall is not endowed like the other colleges. It was named after Edmund Rich of Abingdon, who is believed to have lived and taught on this site

St Edmund Hall n'est pas «doté» comme les autres collèges. Il perpétue la mémoire d'Edmund Rich d'Abingdon, qui avait vécu et enseigné en cet endroit

St Edmund Hall ist keine Stiftung wie die anderen Colleges. Sein Name rührt von Edmund Rich von Abingdon her, der hier an dieser Stelle gelebt und gelehrt haben soll

Hertford: the bridge spanning New College Lane. Hertford, on the site of Hart Hall (1282) belonged to Exeter College for over 400 years. It was later taken over by Magdalen Hall and re-emerged as a separate college in 1874

Hertford: le pont sur New College Lane. Hertford, sur l'emplacement Hart Hall (1282) a appartenu à Exeter College pendant quatre siècles. Il fut ensuite rattaché à Magdalen Hall, puis devint un collège autonome en 1874

Hertford College: die Brücke über New College Lane. Hertford, an der Stelle erbaut, wo früher ein altes Haus namens Hart Hall aus dem Jahre 1282 stand, gehörte über 400 Jahre zu Exeter College. Später wurde es von Magdalen Hall übernommen und ist seit 1874 ein unabhängiges College

St John's: Canterbury Quad, built by William Laud, Archbishop of Canterbury and Chancellor of the University
St John's: Canterbury Quad, bâti par William Laud, archevêque de Canterbury et chancelier de l'Université
St John's: Canterbury-Gebäudehof, von William Laud, Erzbischof von Canterbury und Kanzler der Universität, erbaut

The gateway to the First Quad of St John's. The college was founded in 1555 by Sir Thomas White
L'entrée de First Quad à St John's. Ce collège a été fondé en 1555 par Sir Thomas White
St John's: der Torweg zum Ersten Gebäudehof. Das College wurde 1555 von Sir Thomas White gegründet

The ornate Chapel of Keble, designed by the Victorian architect Butterfield. The college was founded in memory of the poet and pioneer of the Oxford Movement, John Keble

La riche chapelle de Keble, conçue par l'architecte victorien Butterfield. Le collège est dédié à la mémoire du poète John Keble, l'un des fondateurs du «mouvement d'Oxford»

Die reichgeschmückte Kapelle von Keble College, im vorigen Jahrhundert von dem Architekten Butterfield entworfen. Das College wurde zum Andenken an den Dichter und Pionier der Oxford-Bewegung, John Keble, gegründet

The gardens of St Hilda's College for women. This college dates from 1893 and owes its existence to Dorothea Beale, head-
mistress of Cheltenham Ladies' College

Les jardins du collège féminin St Hilda. Ce collège date de 1893 et doit son existence à Dorothée Beale, directrice du Collège
de filles de Cheltenham

Die Gartenanlagen von St Hilda's College für Studentinnen. Es entstand 1893 und verdankt seine Existenz der Direktorin
des Cheltenham Ladies' College, Dorothea Beale

Trinity College was founded in 1554 by Sir Thomas Pope and incorporates some of the old buildings of the Benedictine Durham College. In the background is Exeter College Chapel

Trinity College a été fondé en 1554 par Sir Thomas Pope. Il a hérité de certains bâtiments de l'ancien collège bénédictin de Durham. Au fond, la chapelle d'Exeter College

Trinity College wurde 1554 von Sir Thomas Pope gegründet und umschließt Gebäude des ehemaligen Durham College der Benediktiner. Im Hintergrund die Kapelle von Exeter College

The buildings in the Front Quad of Trinity are mainly 19th century, the work of Sir Thomas Graham Jackson. The college also has a splendid 17th century chapel

Les bâtiments du Front Quad de Trinity sont principalement du XIXᵉ siècle. Ils sont l'oeuvre de Sir Thomas Graham Jackson. Le collège a aussi une très belle chapelle du XVIIᵉ siècle

Die Gebäude des Vorhofs von Trinity stammen in der Hauptsache aus dem 19. Jahrhundert; sie sind das Werk von Sir Thomas Graham Jackson. Das College besitzt eine herrliche Kapelle aus dem 17. Jahrhundert

Merton: general view across Merton Field. Some of the buildings, including the chapel, the library and Mob Quad, date from medieval times

Merton: vue prise de Merton Field. Certains bâtiments, notamment la chapelle, la bibliothèque et Mob Quad, datent du Moyen Age

Merton: Gesamtansicht von Merton Field aus. Einige der Gebäude wie die Kapelle, die Bücherei und „Mob Quad" stammen aus dem Mittelalter

Merton: porter's lodge. Merton claims to be the oldest Oxford college, older even than University College and Balliol. It was founded in 1264 by Walter de Merton, Lord High Chancellor to Henry III

Merton: la loge du portier. Merton revendique le titre de plus ancien collège d'Oxford. Il serait même antérieur à University College et à Balliol. Il fut fondé en 1264 par Walter de Merton, Lord Grand Chancelier d'Henri III

Merton: Pförtnerhaus. Merton rühmt sich, das älteste College in Oxford zu sein, älter sogar als University College und Balliol. Es wurde 1264 von Walter von Merton, Großkanzler Heinrichs III., gegründet

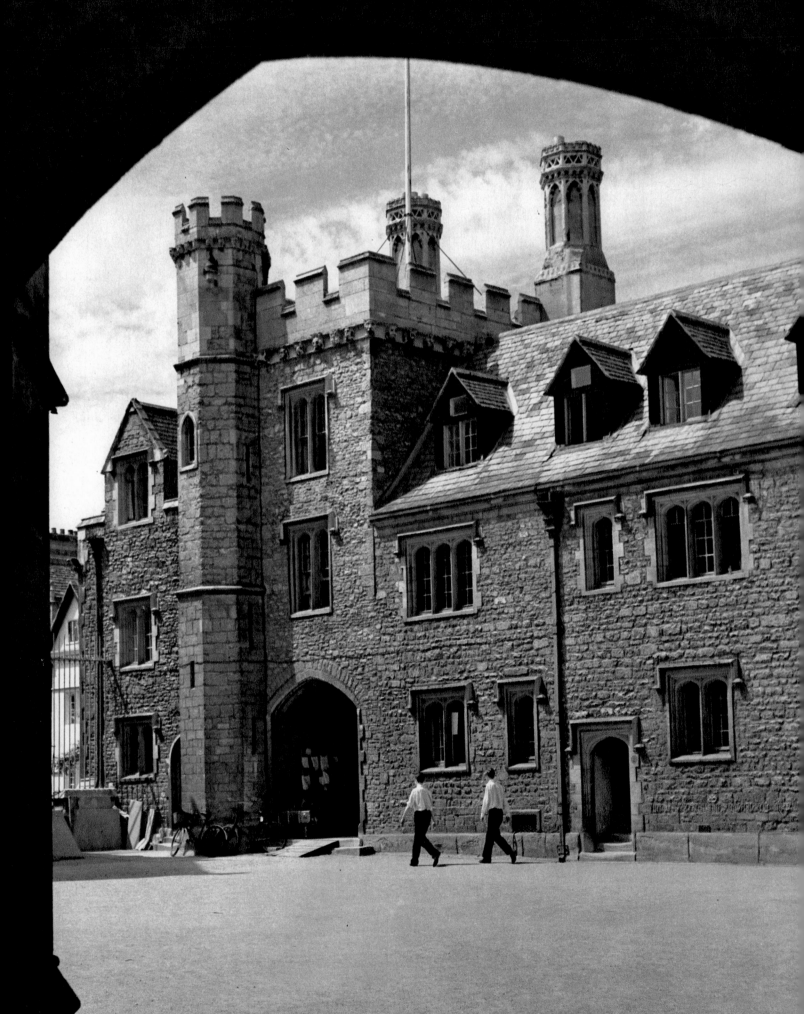

Nuffield: silhouette of tower spire
Nuffield: silhouette du clocher
Nuffield: Silhouette der Turmspitze

56

Nuffield: (left) the quadrangle and (below) the front. The college was founded in 1937 by Lord Nuffield as a post-graduate institution specialising in social studies. It is the only college open both to men and women

Nuffield: (à gauche) la cour carrée, (au-dessous) la façade. Fondé en 1937 par Lord Nuffield pour l'enseignement supérieur des sciences sociales, c'est le seul collège mixte d'Oxford

Hof (links) und Fassade (unten) von Nuffield College. 1937 von Lord Nuffield als Spezialinstitut für Sozialwissenschaften gegründet, ist es das einzige College, das sowohl Männern als auch Frauen offensteht. Alle müssen allerdings schon einen Universitätsgrad besitzen

Jesus College Hall. This was the first Protestant college, founded in 1571 by Queen Elizabeth and Dr Hugh Price, and intended for Welsh students

Jesus College Hall. Ce fut le premier collège protestant, fondé en 1571 par la reine Elizabeth et par le Dr Hugh Price, et destiné aux étudiants gallois

Außenansicht der Hall von Jesus College. Dies war das erste protestantische College, wurde 1571 von Königin Elisabeth und Dr Hugh Price gegründet und war für Studenten aus Wales bestimmt

The University Museum, built by Benjamin Woodward in the mid-19th century, is primarily a natural history museum

Le musée de l'Université, construit par Benjamin Woodward vers 1850, est surtout un musée d'histoire naturelle

Das Universitätsmuseum, von Benjamin Woodward um die Mitte des vorigen Jahrhunderts erbaut, ist in der Hauptsache ein Museum für Naturgeschichte

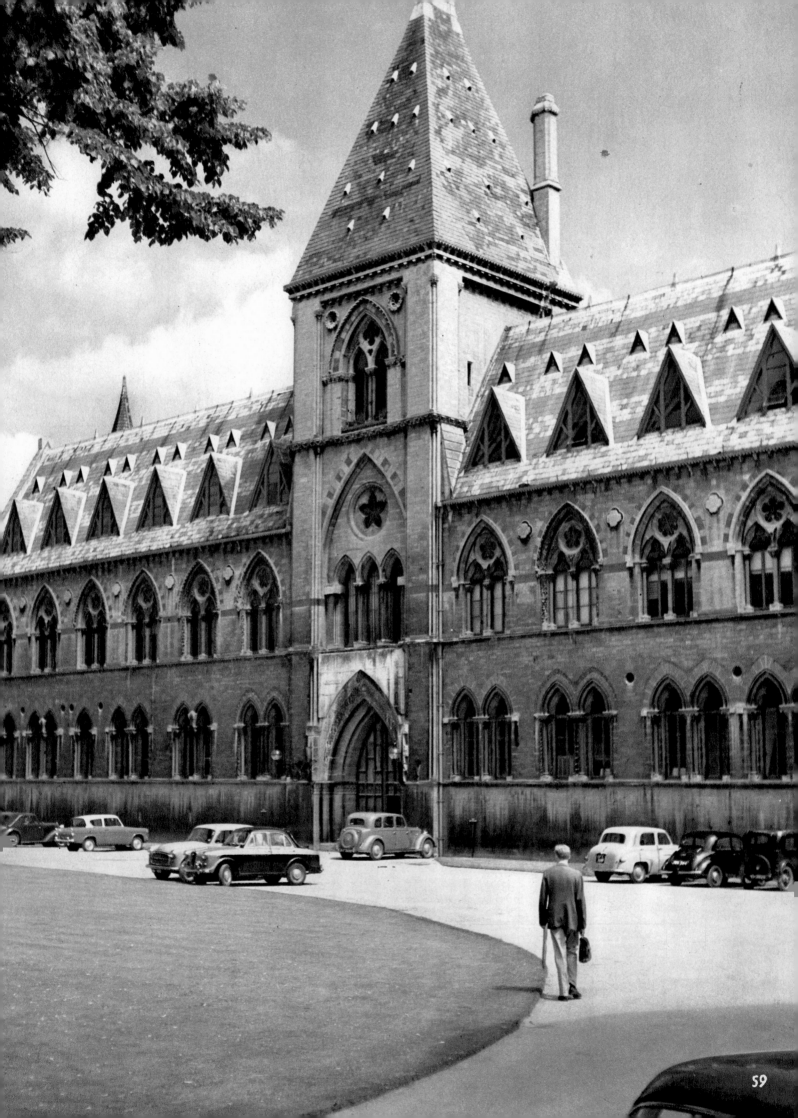

The Ashmolean Museum houses a varied collection of drawings, musical instruments, antiquities, etc. The old museum was opened in 1683 and the present building was erected in 1840

Le musée ashmoléien abrite une riche collection de dessins, d'instruments de musique, d'antiquités, etc. L'ancien musée fut inauguré en 1683; le bâtiment actuel en 1840

Das Ashmolean Museum birgt mannigfaltige Sammlungen von Zeichnungen, Musikinstrumenten, Antiquitäten usw. Das alte Museum wurde 1683 eröffnet; das heutige Gebäude stammt aus dem Jahre 1840

The New Bodleian Library, designed by Sir Giles Gilbert Scott. The old Bodleian Library was built at the beginning of the 17th century to house the original collection of books bequeathed by Sir Thomas Bodley of Merton

La nouvelle bibliothèque Bodley, bâtie sur les plans de Sir Giles Gilbert Scott. L'ancienne bibliothèque du même nom fut construite au début du XVIIe siècle pour abriter la collection léguée par Sir Thomas Bodley de Merton

Die neue Bodleiana, nach dem Entwurf von Sir Giles Gilbert Scott. Die alte Bibliothek war zu Beginn des 17. Jahrhunderts erbaut worden, um die ursprüngliche Sammlung von Büchern, die Sir Thomas Bodley von Merton der Universität hinterlassen hatte, aufzunehmen

Undergraduates outside the University Museum
Etudiants devant le musée de l'Université
Studenten vor dem Universitätsmuseum

A cross-section of undergraduates
Un groupe d'étudiants d'Oxford
Eine typische Studentengruppe

The Radcliffe Camera, near the Bodleian Library, was built by James Gibbs and named after the great Oxford benefactor, Dr John Radcliffe. It is the University's chief reading room

Radcliffe Camera, près de la «bodléienne» fut édifiée par James Gibbs; elle porte le nom du grand bienfaiteur d'Oxford, Dr John Radcliffe. C'est la principale salle de lecture de l'Université

Radcliffe Camera in der Nähe der Bodleiana wurde von James Gibbs erbaut und nach dem großen Wohltäter von Oxford, Dr John Radcliffe, benannt. Es ist der Hauptlesesaal der Universität

Scenes outside the Examination Schools, commonly known as the 'Schools'. Cap, gown and white tie are obligatory for examinations

Devant les «Examination Schools», appelées familièrement les «Schools». Bonnet carré, robe et cravate blanche sont de rigueur pour les examens

Szenen vor den „Schools" genannten Prüfungssälen. Viereckige Kappe, Talar und weißer Schlips sind obligatorisch für Prüfungen

A camera crew at work near Magdalen
Une équipe de cinéastes à l'oeuvre près de Magdalen
Photographen an der Arbeit in der Nähe von Magdalen
College

A leisurely mode of conveyance
Ce moyen de locomotion est bien agréable
Ein gemütliches Beförderungsmittel

Lunchtime snack
Déjeuner sur le pouce
Mittagimbiß

Refills required
«C'est à boire qu'il nous faut . . .»
Gläser, die auf Nachfüllung warten

Christ Church Cathedral: detail of fan-vaulting
Cathédrale de Christ Church: détail des voûtes en éventail
Christ Church: Detail des Fächergewölbes in der Kathedrale

Christ Church Cathedral was originally the church of the Augustinian priory of St Frideswide's
Cathédrale de Christ Church: c'était à l'origine l'église du prieuré augustinien de St Frideswide
Die Kathedrale von Christ Church war ursprünglich die Kirche der Augustinerpriorei St Frideswide

Church of St Mary the Virgin: the Baroque Porch. The spire, completed in 1320, is a famous city landmark

L'église Ste Marie la Vierge: le porche baroque. Le clocher, achevé en 1320, est l'un des plus fameux monuments de la ville

Kirche der Heiligen Jungfrau: die Barockvorhalle. Die Turmspitze aus dem Jahre 1320 ist ein berühmtes Wahrzeichen der Stadt

Church of St Mary the Virgin:
detail of 13th century tower

te Marie la Vierge: détail de la
our du XIIIᵉ siècle

Kirche der Heiligen Jungfrau:
Detail des im 13. Jahrhundert
ntstandenen Turms

71

Church of St Peter in the East. The chancel and
crypt date from the 12th century
St Pierre de l'Est. Le choeur et la crypte datent
du XIIᵉ siècle
Kirche des Heiligen Petrus im Osten. Chor und
Krypta stammen aus dem 12. Jahrhundert

An orchestral rehearsal in progress inside the
church of St Mary the Virgin
Une répétition à Ste Marie la Vierge
Orchesterprobe in der Kirche der Heiligen
Jungfrau

St Martin's Tower, sole remnant of the ancient church which once stood at Carfax in the centre of the town

La tour de St Martin, seul vestige de l'ancienne église qui s'élevait à Carfax, au centre de la ville

Turm des Heiligen Martin, einziges Überbleibsel einer alten Kirche, die einst hier in Carfax im Mittelpunkt der Stadt stand

St. Michael's Church used to stand at the city's north gate. The Saxon tower is the oldest monument in Oxford

L'église St. Michel, autrefois à la porte septentionale de la cité. La Tour saxonne est le plus ancien monument d'Oxford

Die Kirche des Heiligen Michael, ehemals am Nordtor der Stadt. Der sächsische Turm ist Oxfords ältester Zeuge der Vergangenheit

Martyrs' Memorial
Le monument aux Martyrs
Das Märtyrerdenkmal

74

Spire of St Aldate's Church, with reflection of Tom Tower
Le clocher de St Aldate, avec un reflet de Tom Tower
Der Turm der Kirche von St Aldate mit dem Spiegelbild von „Tom Tower"

The Martyrs' Memorial in St Giles's commemorates the burning of Bishops Latimer, Ridley and Cranmer outside the gate of Balliol

Le monument aux Martyrs à St Giles's commémore le martyre des évêques Latimer, Ridley et Cranmer qui furent brûlés devant la porte de Balliol

Das Märtyrerdenkmal in St Giles erinnert an den Feuertod der Bischöfe Latimer, Ridley und Cranmer außerhalb des Tores von Balliol

County Hall
L'hôtel de ville
Das Verwaltungsgebäude der Grafschaft Oxford

The Inorganic Chemistry Laboratory and the Radcliffe Science Library
Le laboratoire de chimie non-organique et la bibliothèque scientifique Radcliffe
Das Laboratorium für anorganische Chemie und die Radcliffe-Bibliothek der Wissenschaften

The Indian Institute is the centre for research on India and Pakistan
L'Institut indien est un centre d'études sur l'Inde et le Pakistan

Das Indische Institut ist der Mittelpunkt für die Indien- und Pakistan- Forschung

The City Library in Blue Boar Street
La bibliothèque municipale, Blue Boar Street
Die Stadtbibliothek in der Blue Boar Street

The War Memorial in St Giles's
Monument aux morts, St Giles's
Das Kriegerdenkmal in St Giles

'Alice's Shop', the original Sheep Shop in Lewis Carroll's 'Through the Looking Glass'
«Alice's Shop», la «Sheep Shop» du célèbre conte de Lewis Carroll, «A Travers le Miroir»
„Alices Laden", das Vorbild des Schafladens in dem Buch von Lewis Carroll „Welt im Spiegel"

Magpie Lane, one of Oxford's lesser known thoroughfares
Magpie Lane, un des carrefours peu connus d'Oxford
Magpie Lane, eine der weniger bekannten Straßen in Oxford

Botanical Gardens and Magdalen Tower. The gardens, begun in 1621, are the oldest of their kind in Europe

Le jardin botanique et la tour Magdalen. Le jardin, commencé en 1621, est le plus ancien de son espèce en Europe

Der botanische Garten und der Turm von Magdalen. Der 1621 angelegte botanische Garten ist der älteste Europas

New College Lane and the towers of All Souls
New College Lane et les tours d'All Souls
New College Lane und die Türme von All Souls

Christ Church Meadow: the Lodge gatehouse
Christ Church Meadow: l'entrée du pavillon de garde
Christ Church Meadow: das Pförtnerhaus

Eights Week: an academic crew
La Semaine des «Huit»: l'une des équipes concurrentes
Woche der Achterrennen: eine Studentenmannschaft

The Isis during Eights Week
L'Isis pendant la Semaine des «Huit»
Die Isis (Themse) während der Woche der Achterrennen

The cox...
Le barreur...
Der Boots-
führer...

Crowded new boathouses during Eights Week
Un aspect du bord de l'eau pendant la Semaine des «Huit»
Die Zuschauermenge auf den neuen Bootshäusern während der Woche der Achterrennen

. . . is ducked
. . . est plongé dans
l'eau
. . . wird getaucht

A river ferry
Un bac
Fähre über den Fluß

A floating clubhouse
Un club flottant
Ein schwimmender Klub

A successful bump during Eights Week
Fin d'une course pendant la Semaine des «Huit»
Erfolgreiches Überholmanöver während der Woche der Achterrennen

CAMBRIDGE

King's College Bridge and Chapel. The college was founded by Henry VI in 1440

King's College. Le pont et la chapelle. Le collège fut fondé par Henri VI en 1440

King's College, Brücke und Kapelle. Das College wurde von Heinrich VI. im Jahre 1440 gegründet

King's College Chapel is indisputably the finest building in Cambridge
La chapelle de King's College est incontestablement le plus bel ouvrage de Cambridge
Die Kapelle von King's College ist ohne Zweifel das schönste Gebäude in Cambridge

Boys from King's College Choir School
De jeunes membres de la chorale de King's College
92 Sängerknaben des Chors von King's College

King's: the Gatehouse and Great Court
King's: le pavillon d'entrée et la grande cour
King's College: Das Torgebäude und der Große Hof 93

King's College Chapel has 25 magnificent stained glass windows depicting scenes from the Old and New Testaments
La chapelle de King's College compte 25 superbes vitraux évoquant des scènes de l'Ancien et du Nouveau Testaments
Die Kapelle von King's College besitzt 25 wunderbare bunte Glasfenster mit Bildern aus dem Alten und Neuen Testament

College porters, with the Chapel in the background
Des portiers du collège, avec la chapelle à l'arrière-plan
Dienstleute mit der Kapelle im Hintergrund

The interior of King's College Chapel is 289 feet long and 80 feet high. The stained glass, the intricate stonework, the carvings and the coats of arms combine to produce an effect of overwhelming beauty

L'intérieur de la chapelle de King's College a 88 mètres de long et 24 mètres de haut. Les vitraux, les dentelles de pierre, les sculptures, les armures composent un ensemble impressionnant

King's College: das Innere der Kapelle ist 88 Meter lang und 24 Meter hoch. Die Glasmalerei der Fenster, die verschlungenen Steinmetzarbeiten, die Schnitz- und Bildhauerwerke und die Wappenschilder bringen zusammen ein Bild überwältigender Schönheit hervor

The roof of King's College Chapel is one of the finest examples of fan-vaulting in England; about 2 miles of narrow stone ribbons were employed

Le toit de la chapelle de King's College est l'un des plus beaux exemples de voûte en éventail qu'on puisse voir en Angleterre; il y a là environ 3 kilomètres de minces rubans de pierre

Das Dachwerk der Kapelle von King's College ist eines der schönsten Fächergewölbe in England. Die schmalen Steinrippen wären aneinandergelegt ungefähr drei Kilometer lang

King's Parade, outside King's College
King's Parade, devant King's College
King's Parade, außerhalb King's College

Cambridge rooftops, from Church of St Mary the Great
Les toits de Cambridge, vu de l'église Ste Marie la grande
Die Dächer von Cambridge, von der Kirche St Mary the Great aus gesehen

The Great Gate of Trinity College. The founder of the college was Henry VIII (1546)

La grande porte de Trinity College. Le fondateur du collège (1546) fut Henri VIII

Das Große Tor von Trinity College. Der Gründer des Colleges war Heinrich VIII. (1546)

Statue of Henry VIII on Great Gate. The object in the right hand is of recent date

Statue d'Henri VIII, face à la grande porte. L'objet qu'il tient à la main droite n'est pas ancien

Das Standbild Heinrichs VIII. am Großen Tor. Der Gegenstand in seiner rechten Hand ist neueren Ursprungs

Trinity's Wren Library, seen from the Backs. Built between 1675 and 1690, the Library contains many literary treasures

La bibliothèque Wren, à Trinity, vue des «Backs». Construite de 1675 à 1690, la bibliothèque contient de nombreux manuscrits et ouvrages précieux

Die Wren-Bibliothek von Trinity, von den „Backs" aus gesehen. Die zwischen 1675 und 1690 erbaute Bibliothek enthält viele literarische Kostbarkeiten

The Hall of Trinity College in the Great Court is designed on the model of London's Middle Temple and is the largest in Cambridge

Le Hall de Trinity College, dans la grande cour, est imité de Middle Temple à Londres. C'est le plus grand de Cambridge

Die Hall von Trinity College, die größte in Cambridge, ist nach dem Vorbild des Londoner „Middle Temple" entworfen

The Great Court of Trinity, with the Clock-tower, Chapel and Fountain. This is the largest of all the Oxford and Cambridge quadrangles and courts

La grande cour de Trinity, avec la tour de l'horloge, la chapelle et la fontaine. C'est la plus grande de toutes les cours d'Oxford et de Cambridge

Der Große Hof von Trinity mit dem Uhrturm, der Kapelle und dem Springbrunnen. Dies ist der größte aller Collegehöfe in Oxford und Cambridge

Trinity: statues in Antechapel. In the foreground is Francis Bacon, and the standing figure is Sir Isaac Newton; both men studied at Trinity. The third statue is of Dr Isaac Barrow

Trinity: statues de l'avant corps de la chapelle. Au premier plan, Francis Bacon et, debout, Sir Isaac Newton; tous deux furent étudiants à Trinity. La troisième statue représente Dr Isaac Barrow

Trinity: Standbilder in der Vorhalle zur Kapelle. Die Figur im Vordergrund ist Francis Bacon, die aufrechtstehende weiter hinten Sir Isaac Newton; beide waren Studenten von Trinity. Die dritte Statue stellt Dr Isaac Barrow dar

Trinity's New Court is a 19th century addition

La nouvelle cour de Trinity est une innovation du XIXᵉ siècle

Der Neue Hof in Trinity ist eine Hinzufügung des 19. Jahrhunderts

The 'Bridge of Sighs', which links St John's Library with New Court
Le «Pont des soupirs», qui relie la bibliothèque de St John's à la nouvelle cour
Die „Seufzerbrücke" zwischen der Bibliothek von St John's und dem Neuen Hof

The Great Gate of St John's, with a statue of Lady Margaret Beaufort, who founded the college in 1511

La grande porte de St John's, avec une statue de Lady Margaret Beaufort, qui fonda le collège en 1511

Das Große Tor von St John's mit der Statue von Lady Margaret Beaufort, Gründerin des Colleges im Jahre 1511

The Beaufort arms on the Great Gate are supported by strange heraldic beasts called yales

Les armes de la maison de Beaufort, sur la grande porte, sont soutenues par d'étranges animaux héraldiques appelés «yales»

Das Wappen der Beauforts am Großen Tor wird von seltsamen heraldischen, „Yales" genannten Tieren gehalten

The tower of St John's Chapel, which was designed by Sir Gilbert Scott
La tour de la chapelle de St John's, oeuvre de Sir Gilbert Scott
Der Turm der Kapelle von St John's, entworfen von Sir Gilbert Scott

Punts entangled on the Backs
Emmêlement de bateux sur les «Backs»
Ein Knäuel von Flachbooten an den ,,Backs"

The Backs, with a view of St John's New Court
Les «Backs», avec une vue sur la nouvelle cour de St John's
Die ,,Backs" mit dem Neuen Hof von St John's im Hintergrund

Gonville and Caius is traditionally a medical college, founded as Gonville Hall in 1348, and as a college by Dr John Caius in 1557

Gonville and Caius, traditionnellement collège de médecine; Gonville Hall (1348) devint un collège grâce à la dotation du Dr John Caius en 1557

Gonville and Caius College ist traditionsgemäß das College für Mediziner. 1348 als Gonville Hall gegründet, wurde es 1557 durch Dr John Caius zum College

The Gate of Honour at Gonville and Caius, through which students pass to receive their degrees

La porte d'honneur de Gonville and Caius, par laquelle passent les étudiants pour aller recevoir leur diplôme

Das Ehrentor von Gonville and Caius, durch das Studenten passieren, wenn sie ihren akademischen Grad empfangen

Peterhouse, founded in 1284 by Hugh de Balsham,
Bishop of Ely, is the oldest college in Cambridge

Peterhouse, fondé en 1284 par Hugues de Balsham,
évêque d'Ely, est le plus ancien collège de Cambridge

Peterhouse, 1284 von Hugh von Balsham, Bischof von
Ely, gegründet, ist das älteste College in Cambridge

A rooftop view of Gonville and Caius, with St John's
Chapel in background

Vue aérienne de Gonville and Caius, avec la chapelle
de St John's à l'arrière-plan

Gonville and Caius, von einem Nachbardach aus gesehen, mit der Kapelle von St John's im Hintergrund

The Pepys Library. The date, 1724, refers to the year when the collection was transferred to the college on the death of Pepys's nephew, John Jackson

La bibliothèque Pepys. La date, 1724, commémore l'année où la collection fut transférée au collège à la mort du neveu de Pepys, John Jackson

Die Pepys-Bibliothek. Das Datum 1724 bezieht sich auf das Jahr, in dem die Bücherei nach dem Tode von John Jackson, dem Neffen von Pepys, dem College einverleibt wurde

Magdalene: the Pepys Library. Samuel Pepys bequeathed to his college his precious collection of 3,000 books, including the 'Diary'

Magdalene: la bibliothèque Pepys. Samuel Pepys légua à son collège sa précieuse collection de 3,000 livres, comprenant son fameux «Journal»

Magdalene: die Pepys-Bibliothek. Der Schriftsteller Samuel Pepys vermachte seinem College seine kostbare Sammlung von 3,000 Bänden, einschließlich seines berühmten „Tagebuchs"

Residential quarters at Magdalene. The college stands on the site of a Benedictine hostel and was founded in 1542 by Thomas Lord Audley, Chancellor to Henry VIII

Maisons d'étudiants à Magdalene. Le collège, situé sur l'emplacement d'un ancien hôtel bénédictin, fut fondé en 1542 par Thomas Lord Audley, chancelier d'Henri VIII

Studentenwohnungen in Magdalene. Thomas Lord Audley, Kanzler Heinrichs VIII., gründete das College 1542 an der Stelle, auf der früher eine Herberge der Benediktiner stand

Wrought-iron gates at Magdalene. Although a small college, Magdalene boasts many eminent former students, such as Charles Kingsley and Charles Stewart Parnell

Les grilles de fer forgé de Magdalene. Malgré sa petite taille, Magdalene se flatte d'avoir compté maints étudiants de grand talent, comme Charles Kingsley et Charles Stewart Parnell

Das schmiedeeiserne Tor von Magdalene. Obwohl es nur ein kleines College ist, kann Magdalene sich vieler bedeutender Studenten rühmen, wie zum Beispiel Charles Kingsley und Charles Stewart Parnell

The 14th century Old Court at Corpus Christi is the oldest in Cambridge
L'ancienne cour de Corpus Christi (XIVᵉ siècle) est la plus ancienne de Cambridge
Der aus dem 14. Jahrhundert stammende Alte Hof von Corpus Christi ist der älteste in Cambridge

Mallory Court, Magdalene, with St John's Chapel on right
Mallory Court, Magdalene, avec la chapelle de St John's à droite
Mallory-Hof, Magdalene, mit der Kapelle von St John's rechts

Corpus Christi: the Chapel. The college was founded in 1352 by the Gilds of Corpus Christi and St Mary
La chapelle de Corpus Christi. Le collège fut fondé en 1352 par les guildes de Corpus Christi et de Ste Marie
Corpus Christi: die Kapelle. Das College wurde 1352 von den Gilden von Corpus Christi und St Mary gegründet

Interior of Corpus Christi Chapel, built in the 19th century
L'intérieur de la chapelle de Corpus Christi, construite au XIXᵉ siècle
Das Innere der im 19. Jahrhundert gebauten Kapelle von Corpus Christi

The Newton Sundial over the old chapel in Queens' First Court. The association with Newton is dubious since the sundial was built in 1642, the year of the great scientist's birth

Le cadran solaire Newton, sur la vieille chapelle de la première cour, à Queens'. L'attribution à Newton est douteuse, car le cadran fut construit en 1642, année de la naissance du grand savant

Newton-Sonnenuhr an der ehemaligen Kapelle im Ersten Hof von Queens'. Eine Verbindung mit Newton ist nicht sehr wahrscheinlich, da die Sonnenuhr aus dem Jahre 1642 stammt, dem Geburtsjahr des großen Wissenschaftlers

Queens': wooden bridge on the Backs. The college was founded in 1448 by Andrew Dokett; the Queens were Margaret of Anjou, wife of Henry VI, and Elizabeth Woodville, wife of Edward IV

Queens': pont de bois sur les «Backs». Le collège fut fondé en 1448 par Andrew Dokett; les reines du titre du collège étaient Marguerite d'Anjou, femme d'Henri VI, et Elizabeth Woodville, femme d'Edouard IV

Queens': Holzbrücke an den „Backs". Andrew Dokett stiftete das College im Jahre 1448; die Königinnen, nach denen es benannt ist, waren Margaret von Anjou, die Frau Heinrichs VI., und Elisabeth Woodville, die Frau Eduards IV.

The Gateway of Christ's College, with the Beaufort coat of arms. Christ's was founded in 1448 by Lady Margaret Beaufort and her son Henry VI. John Milton was a student here

L'entrée de Christ's College, avec l'armure de Beaufort. Christ's fut fondé en 1448 par Lady Margaret Beaufort et son fils Henri VI. John Milton y fut étudiant

Der Torweg von Christ's College mit dem Beaufort-Wappenschild. Christ's wurde 1448 von Lady Margaret Beaufort und ihrem Sohn Heinrich VI. gegründet. John Milton studierte hier

Queens': Cloister Court and President's Lodge. The court is one of the most attractive in Cambridge, with well-preserved timbered buildings

Queens': la cour du cloître et la loge du Président. La cour est l'une des plus charmantes de Cambridge avec ses maisons de bois bien conservées

Queens': Kreuzganghof und Präsidentenhaus. Der Hof mit seinen ausgezeichnet erhaltenen Fachwerkgebäuden ist einer der fesselndsten in Cambridge

The 17th century court of St. Catherine's, a college founded by Dr. Robert Woodlarke in 1473

La cour de St. Catherine's (XVIIᵉ siècle), collège fondé en 1473 par le Dr. Robert Woodlarke

Der Hof von St Catherine's College, das 1473 von Dr Robert Woodlarke gegründet wurde, stammt aus dem 17. Jahrhundert

Newnham: bronze gates. Opened as a house in 1871, Newnham became a recognised women's college in 1948

Newnham: portes de bronze. Simple habitation à l'origine (1871), Newnham devint un collège féminin en 1948

Newnham: Bronzetor. 1871 eröffnet, wurde Newnham 1948 als ein College für Studentinnen anerkannt

Downing College is built in the Greek style, started by William Wilkins in 1807 and completed during this century. The founder was Sir George Downing who died in 1749, and the Charter was only granted in 1800

Downing College est construit dans le style grec. Commencé par William Wilkins en 1807, il fut achevé beaucoup plus tard. Son fondateur, Sir George Downing, mourut en 1749. La charte ne fut accordée qu'en 1800

William Wilkins begann den Bau von Downing College im griechischen Stil im Jahre 1807; erst im 20. Jahrhundert wurde es fertiggestellt. Der Stifter war Sir George Downing, der 1749 starb. Die Gründungsurkunde wurde erst im Jahre 1800 anerkannt

First Court of Emmanuel College, founded by Sir Walter Mildmay in 1584. John Harvard, who gave his name to the great American university, studied here, and the college is much visited by Americans

La première cour d'Emmanuel College, fondé par Sir Walter Mildmay en 1584. John Harvard, qui donna son nom à la grande université américaine, y fut étudiant. Aussi le collège reçoit-il de nombreux visiteurs d'Amérique

Emmanuel College: der Erste Hof. John Harvard, der der großen amerikanischen Universität den Namen gab, studierte hier in diesem von Sir Walter Mildmay 1584 gegründeten College, das viel von Amerikanern besucht wird

Jesus: the Gate Tower and the high walled path known as the 'Chimney'

Jesus: la tour de l'entrée et l'allée bordée de murs élevés, appelée «la cheminée»

Jesus: der Torweg und der von hohen Mauern umschlossene, allgemein als „Kamin" bekannte Zugang. Der Gründer von Jesus College war John Alcock, Bishof von Ely, im Jahre 1496

Clare, founded as University Hall in 1326, is the second oldest Cambridge college. This is Memorial Court

Clare, à l'origine University Hall (1326), est l'un des deux plus anciens collèges de Cambridge. On voit ici la cour du mémorial

Clare, 1326 als University Hall errichtet, ist das zweitälteste College in Cambridge. Das Bild stellt den Gedächtnishof dar

The Chapel of Selwyn College, founded in 1882 in memory of George Selwyn, first Bishop of New Zealand

La chapelle de Selwyn College, fondé en 1882 à la mémoire de George Selwyn, premier évêque de Nouvelle-Zélande

Die Kapelle von Selwyn College, 1882 erbaut zum Andenken an George Selwyn, den ersten Bischof von Neuseeland

Sidney Sussex College Chapel. This is a college named after Frances Sidney, Countess of Sussex
La chapelle de Sidney Sussex College. Ce collège porte le nom de Frances Sidney, comtesse de Sussex
Die Kapelle von Sidney Sussex. Dies ist ein College, das seinen Namen nach Frances Sidney, Gräfin von Sussex, erhalten hat

The Wren Chapel at Pembroke was the famous architect's first building

La chapelle Wren à Pembroke, première oeuvre du
célèbre architecte

Die von Wren erbaute Kapelle von Pembroke war die
erste Schöpfung des später berühmt gewordenen Architekten

Pembroke was founded in 1347 and named after
Mary de Saint Paul, Countess of Pembroke

Pembroke, fondé en 1347, perpétue le nom de
Marie de Saint Paul, comtesse de Pembroke

Pembroke, 1347 gegründet, erhielt seinen Namen
nach Mary de Saint Paul, Gräfin von Pembroke

Garret Hostel Bridge and Trinity Hall, a college long associated with the legal profession
Garret Hostel Bridge et Trinity Hall, collège où se forment traditionnellement les gens de robe
Garret Hostel Bridge und Trinity Hall, ein College das traditionell das Rechtsstudium pflegt

Student life . . .
La vie des étudiants . . .
Studentenleben . . .

. . . the universal conveyance
. . . un moyen de locomotion traditionnel
. . . der Universaltransport

... women get away with anything
... les femmes arrivent toujours à leurs fins
... „Fahrräder verboten", aber Frauen können sich alles erlauben

For display
Exposition
Nur zum Ansehen

For sale
A vendre
Nur zum Verkauf

138

Relaxing after exams
Après l'examen
Einen Augenblick frische Luft nach der Prüfung

Senate House is the seat of University government, where all ceremonial functions are held
Senate House est le siège de l'université, où se tiennent toutes les cérémonies officielles
Senate House, der Sitz der Universitätsbehörden, wo alle Zeremonien und Feierlichkeiten stattfinden

Market Hill and Church of St Mary the Great
Market Hill et l'église Ste Marie la grande
Market Hill und die Kirche von St Mary the Great

King's Parade, Senate House and Church of St Mary the Great
King's Parade, Senate House et Ste Marie la grande
King's Parade, Senate House und die Kirche St Mary the Great

Two views of the modern Chemical Laboratories in Lensfield Road
Deux vues des laboratoires de chimie, dans Lensfield Road
Zwei Ansichten der modernen Chemischen Laboratorien in Lensfield Road

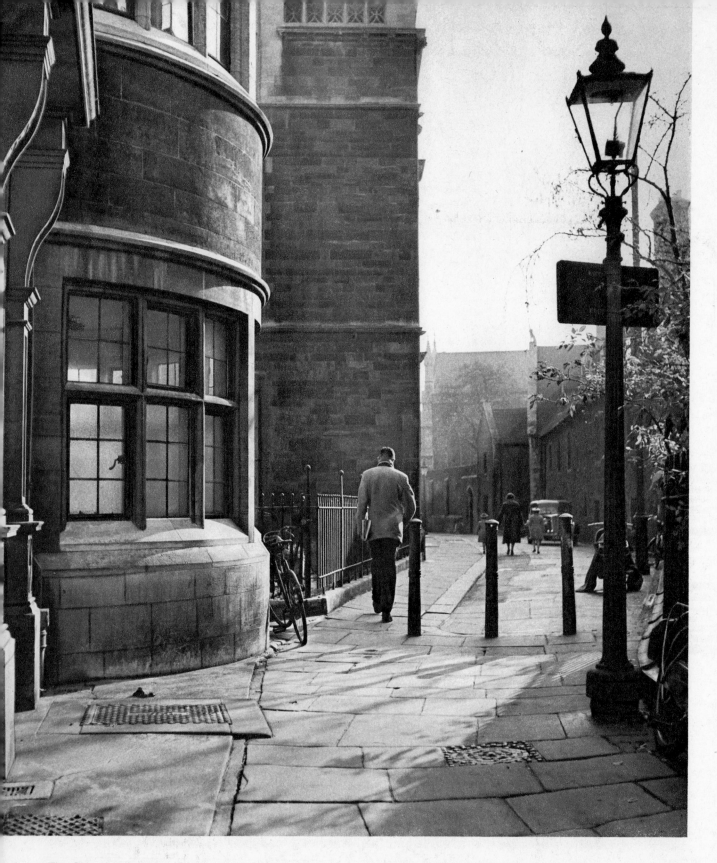

The Cavendish Laboratory, specialising in physics, where the first experiments in nuclear fission took place
Le laboratoire Cavendish de physique où eurent lieu les premières expériences de fission nucléaire
Das Cavendish-Laboratorium, wo die ersten Kernphysik-Experimente stattfanden

Little St Mary Lane

Hobson's Conduit, at the corner of Lensfield Road, commemorates the famous carrier, Thomas Hobson, who perpetuated the phrase 'Hobson's Choice'

Hobson's Conduit, au coin de Lensfield Road, commémore le fameux roulier Thomas Hobson

Hobson's Conduit, an der Ecke der Lensfield Road errichtet zum Andenken an den berühmten Transportunternehmer Thomas Hobson

The University Press, from St Botolph's Church. Both Universities have an honourable tradition of printing and publishing
University Press, vue de l'église St. Botolphe. Les deux universités ont illustré l'histoire de l'impression et de l'édition
University Press, von der St-Botolphs-Kirche gesehen. Die Universitäten von Oxford und Cambridge können auf eine
ehrenvolle Tätigkeit als Drucker und Verleger zurückschauen

Statue, by Captain Scott's widow, in the garden of the Scott Polar Research Institute
Statue, due à la veuve du capitaine Scott, dans le jardin de l'Institut de recherches polaires Scott
Statue, gestiftet von der Witwe Kapitän Scotts, im Garten des Scott-Instituts für Polarforschung

Modern statuary in Clare Memorial Court
Statue moderne dans la cour de Clare College
Moderne Skulptur im Gedächtnishof von Clare College

Farnese Herakles, in the Museum of Classical Archaeology
Hercule Farnèse, au Musée d'archéologie classique
Der Farnesische Herakles im Museum für klassische Archäologie

St Benedict's Church, with its typically Saxon tower
St Benoît, avec sa tour saxonne caractéristique
Die Kirche St Benedikt mit ihrem typischen sächsischen Turm

Church of the Holy Sepulchre, the oldest of the four existing English round churches
L'église du Saint Sépulchre, la plus ancienne des quatre églises rondes d'Angleterre
Die Kirche des Heiligen Grabes, die älteste der vier Rundkirchen in England

151

Church of St Mary the Less: the splendid Early English East window

L'église Ste Marie la petite: le très beau vitrail anglais de style ancien

Kirche St Mary the Less: das wundervolle gotische Ostfenster

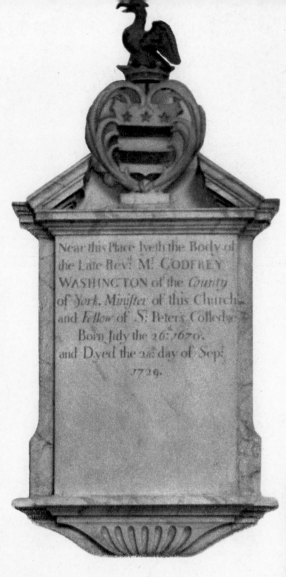

Church of St Mary the Less: the Washington family arms, showing the origin of the American national emblem

L'église Ste Marie la petite: les armes de la famille Washington, où l'on trouve les origines de l'emblème national des Etats-Unis

Kirche St Mary the Less: das Wappen der Familie Washington, das den Ursprung des Emblems Amerikas zeigt

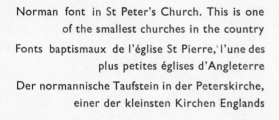

Norman font in St Peter's Church. This is one of the smallest churches in the country

Fonts baptismaux de l'église St Pierre, l'une des plus petites églises d'Angleterre

Der normannische Taufstein in der Peterskirche, einer der kleinsten Kirchen Englands

153

Cambridge lets its hair down at the traditional Poppy Day Rag
Un peu de fantasie pour la fête de l'armistice
Am Waffenstillstandstag läßt Cambridge sich gehen

154

Poppy Day Rag: original and uninhibited ways of raising money

Quelques moyens originaux de faire la quête le jour de la fête de l'armistice

Man greift zu den originellsten und hemmungs-losesten Mitteln, um am Waffenstillstandstag Geld zu sammeln

Parish Church of St Andrew, Chesterton
Eglise paroissiale St André, Chesterton
Die Pfarrkirche St Andrew in Chesterton

The millpond at Grantchester, a village which has inspired many poets
Le réservoir du moulin à Grantchester, village qui à inspiré de nombreux poètes
Der Mühlteich in Grantchester, einem Dorf, das viele Dichter begeistert hat

Coe Fen